3 Stories in one

BIBLE HEROES
STORYBOOK

- Mary Visits Elizabeth
- Jesus Grows Up
- Jesus and Lazarus

MARY VISITS ELIZABETH

Retold by Andy Rector

Illustrated by Ben Mahan

Zechariah entered the temple. As a priest, he had the duty of burning incense to the Lord. The people waited outside of the temple as Zechariah completed his duties. Suddenly an angel appeared to Zechariah.

"You and your wife Elizabeth have no children," said the angel, "but the Lord has sent me to tell you that Elizabeth will have a son."

"But we are old," said Zechariah. "How can that be possible?"

The angel said, "I am Gabriel, a messenger of the Lord. Since you do not believe the Lord's word, you will be speechless until your son is born." Then Gabriel left.

When Zechariah walked outside the people wondered, "What is wrong with him? Why can't he talk?"

Soon the people realized Zechariah had seen a vision.

Later, in a town nearby, Mary worked in her house. She was sweeping the floor when a bright angel suddenly appeared in the room. Mary trembled and dropped to her knees at the strange sight of the angel.

"Don't be afraid, Mary," said Gabriel. "The Lord has chosen you to have His son whose name will be Jesus. He will

be a great and wonderful man."

"How can this be?" said Mary.

"Everything is possible with the Lord," said Gabriel. "The Lord will cause your relative, Elizabeth, who could not have children, to have a son also."

"I will serve the Lord," said Mary. Then Gabriel left her.

When Mary heard Elizabeth would have a son, she packed a few items and walked to the town where Zechariah and Elizabeth lived.

Soon Mary saw Elizabeth in the distance, standing outside of her house. Mary waved and Elizabeth waved back. "Hello, Elizabeth," said Mary, and they hugged. "So good to see you," Mary told Elizabeth.

"The Lord said I am to have a son," said Elizabeth.

"He has said the same to me," said Mary. "Our sons will have a special purpose for serving the Lord."

"Yes," Elizabeth said, placing her hand on her stomach. " I can already feel the child. When I heard you call my name, the baby leaped for joy inside me. He knows your baby is the Savior."

Mary stayed with Elizabeth for a few months before

going home. The time came for Elizabeth to have her baby. Just as the angel had said, the baby was a boy.

"What will his name be?" people asked.

"John," said Zechariah. It was the first time he had spoken since Gabriel's visit. And so the baby's name became John.

Meanwhile, Mary prayed every day in her little house. She thought about the visit of the angel and wondered why the Lord had picked her to be the mother of the Savior. "Dear Lord," she prayed, "I know with you all things are possible. I am a little nervous and confused about the things that will happen, but I trust You will protect me and make things work out right."

JESUS GROWS UP

Retold by Andy Rector

Illustrated by Ben Mahan

After Mary had her baby, she and her new husband, Joseph, went to the temple to show their son to the priests.

When Mary and Joseph walked into the temple, an old man named Simeon came over and took the baby Jesus out of Mary's arms.

"The Holy Spirit told me," said Simeon, "that I would live to see the Savior. Today the Spirit told me this baby is the Savior. I have waited many years for this day to happen."

As Simeon walked away, Joseph and Mary looked at each other. They were amazed at all the things being said about their special baby.

Jesus grew into a wise young boy. Once a year Joseph, Mary and many other friends and relatives walked to a town called Jerusalem to worship the Lord in a feast known as Passover. When Jesus was twelve, they took such a trip.

Many people walked together down the roads until they reached Jerusalem. After the feast of Passover was celebrated, Mary and Joseph began to walk home with everyone else. "Where is Jesus?" asked Mary.

"Oh, he is probably walking with his friends," Joseph replied. They searched the crowd, but could not find Jesus.

Mary and Joseph looked and looked until they finally found Jesus in the temple in Jerusalem. Jesus sat with all the teachers talking with them about the scriptures. The teachers were amazed at his wisdom.

"Jesus," said Mary. "Why are you here?" You have worried us."

'Didn't you know," Jesus said, "that I had to be in my Father's house?" They didn't understand what he meant.

Jesus grew into a strong and wise man. Mary knew her son had been chosen by the Lord to do special things, but most people in town just thought of Jesus as a nice man.

John, Elizabeth's son and a cousin of Jesus, was a bit different. He wore clothes made out of camel hair tied with a leather belt. He wandered around the countryside eating locusts and wild honey.

They called him John the Baptist because he would preach to the crowds about God, and baptize people in the water.

One day Jesus walked up to the crowds standing around John the Baptist.

"Here he comes," said John. "It's Jesus, the Savior."

"Baptize me," said Jesus to John.

"But you are the Savior. You don't need to be baptized."

"This is the Lord's will," Jesus said.

So John took Jesus down into the Jordan River and baptized him. As Jesus came out of the water, the sky opened up. A white dove flew down and landed on the shoulder of Jesus.

Suddenly everyone around heard a voice from the sky: "You are my son, whom I love, with you I am well pleased." God had spoken to Jesus, His only son.

JESUS and LAZARUS

Retold by Andy Rector

Illustrated by Ben Mahan

In a little town called Bethany there were two sisters named Mary and Martha; they had a brother named Lazarus. Jesus visited the three often and they liked to consider Jesus their best friend.

One day Lazarus became sick.

"I don't think he is going to live much longer," Martha said to Mary.

"We must send someone to get Jesus," said Mary.

"Yes," Martha said. "I'm sure Jesus will be able to help Lazarus get better."

Jesus was in another town preaching about the word of God. As he was speaking one day, a man approached him suddenly.

"Jesus!"

"Yes, my friend, what is it?" Jesus answered.

"I am a friend of Mary and Martha. They asked me to come here and to bring you back to their house. Lazarus is very sick."

"This sickness will not end in death," said Jesus. "He has become sick for a reason. This is a way to show the glory of God's power."

But Jesus did not leave his preaching right away. In fact he continued to do the Lord's work for two more days in the town where he received the message about Lazarus. Only then did he leave for Bethany.

By the time Jesus arrived in Bethany, Lazarus had already died. His body had been buried in a tomb for four days.

Martha ran out to greet Jesus. She said, "Jesus, if you had been here, Lazarus would not have died. But I know God will do whatever you ask."

Jesus said to her, "Your brother will rise again."

Martha did not exactly understand what Jesus meant. She said, "Yes, it is true, when we all go to heaven Lazarus will be there in a new life."

Jesus smiled. "I am the resurrection. Whoever believes in me will live forever. Do you believe in me, Martha?"

"Yes my Lord. I believe you are the Christ."

"Let me speak to your sister, Mary," said Jesus.

Martha went into the house to get Mary.

"Jesus is looking for you," said Martha. Mary got up and ran outside to see Jesus. Some friends and neighbors had

stopped by to comfort Martha and Mary. When they saw Mary running outside, they followed her.

Mary was crying and all the friends of Lazarus were crying too. Jesus was saddened by all these tears of sorrow and he also cried.

"Where is the body of Lazarus?" asked Jesus.

Mary and Martha led Jesus to the tomb where the body of Lazarus lay.

"Remove the stone," said Jesus.

"The glory of God will be shown through the death of Lazarus," said Jesus. The stone was moved. Jesus spoke in a loud voice. "Lazarus, come out!"

People gasped, Mary and Martha could not believe their eyes. Lazarus came walking out of the tomb. He was alive!

That night Jesus celebrated with Mary, Martha and Lazarus. "We all believe you are the Christ," they said. "Thanks be to God."